SRA Reading Mastery Plus

Workbook C

Level 1

A Division of The McGraw·Hill Companies

Columbus, Ohio

Illustration Credits

Loretta Lustig, Jan Pyk

www.sra4kids.com

SRA/McGraw-Hill

*A Division of The **McGraw·Hill** Companies*

Send all inquiries to:
SRA/McGraw-Hill
8787 Orion Place
Columbus, OH 43240-4027

Printed in the United States of America.

ISBN 0-07-569022-5

6 7 8 9 POH 06 05

stōry Ītems

1. arf was a barking _____.

   • card   • shark   • farm

2. a big _____ swam up to the other sharks.

   • fish   • fin   • fan

---

shē is in a car.
she is in a car.

---

n ___ ___ ___ ___

u ___ ___ ___ ___

m ___ ___ ___ ___

h ___ ___ ___ ___

w ___ ___ ___ ___

v ___ ___ ___ ___

rēadiṅg

a boy āte cāke.

hē got sick.

1. a ▬▬▬ āte cāke.

- man   • boy   • girl

2. hē got ▬▬▬.

- sick   • sad   • wet

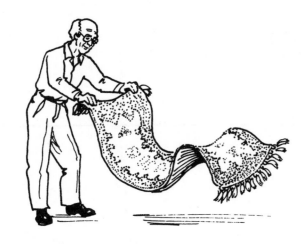

1. this **m**_____ is ōld.

2. hē has a **r**_____.

1. the **b**_____ is in
   the trēē

2. the **p**_____ is in
   the trēē.

story Items

1. arf had to ▬▬▬ the other sharks.

   • hēar   • help   • hōld

2. arf swam up to the big ▬▬▬ .

   • farm   • fat   • fish

3. do the other sharks līke arf now?

   • yes   • nō

---

arf was a shark.

arf was a shark.

---

h _ _ _ _   i _ _ _ _

n _ _ _ _   a _ _ _ _

m _ _ _ _   o _ _ _ _

rēadiṇg

wē ran in the rāin.

wē had wet fēēt.

1. wē ran in the ▬▬▬▬.

   • rōad   • rāin   • lāke

2. ▬▬▬▬ had wet fēēt.

   • you   • mē   • wē

1. the **d**▬▬▬▬ is gōiṇg for the pig.

2. that pig has a **h**▬▬▬▬.

1. a **m**▬▬▬▬ is in the car.

2. a **p**▬▬▬▬ is on the car.

rēadinͤg

fīve fish went fōr a swim.

they met a shark nāmed arf.

1. fīve fish went ▬▬▬▬.

   - to a lāke   • fōr a fish

   - fōr a swim

2. they met a ▬▬▬▬.

   - ship   • bark   • shark

---

a farmer had an ōld cow.

the farmer sat, and the cow went to slēēp.

1. a farmer had an ▬▬▬▬.

   - ōld hat   • ōld cow   • ōld how

2. the cow ▬▬▬▬.

   - sat   • went to the farm

   - went to slēēp

1. the girl got a **h** _____ .

2. the **b** _____

   is **m** _____ .

h _ _ _ _

i _ _ _ _

J _ _ _ _

k _ _ _ _

l _ _ _ _

m _ _ _ _

arf can swim far.

stōry Ītems

1. a cow boy did not have a ▭▭▭.

     ● cow   ● hat   ● hōrse

2. then the cow boy got on a ▭▭▭.

     ● cow   ● cat   ● car

3. the other cow boys said, "▭▭▭."

     ● gō, gō   ● hō, hō   ● nō, nō

he had a cow.

s ___ ___ ___   f ___ ___ ___

t ___ ___ ___   l ___ ___ ___

r ___ ___ ___   i ___ ___ ___

the girls ran with a dog. the dog

ran and ran. the girls had to stop.

1. the girls ran with a ▃▃▃▃.

- dog   - gōat   - man

2. the ▃▃▃▃ had to stop.

- men   - girls   - dog

---

a farmer had a cow. the cow had

a pet. the pet was a bug.

1. a farmer had a ▃▃▃▃.

- bell   - cow   - bug

2. the cow had a pet ▃▃▃▃.

- but   - dog   - bug

1. the man has big **f**▃▃▃▃.

2. the girl has a **h**▃▃▃▃.

stŌry Ītems

1. the cow boys rŌde to a ▬▬▬.

   • lāke   • pond   • crēēk

2. a cow boy's hŌrse ▬▬▬.

   • stoppεd   • slid   • jumpεd

3. the cow boy on the cow said, "▬▬▬."

   • hŌ, hŌ   • nŌ, nŌ   • sŌ, sŌ

a cow boy fell.

d _ _ _ _   a _ _ _ _

v _ _ _   u _ _ _ _

o _ _ _ _   i _ _ _

a bug got mad at a cat. the bug said,

"I will bīte you." sō the bug bit the cat.

1. a _____ got mad at a cat.

   • ran   • cat   • bug

2. sō the bug _____ the cat.

   • bīte   • hit   • bit

I went to slēēp in a barn. a cow

kissed mȳ hand. I līke that cow.

1. I went to _____ in a barn.

   • run   • sit   • slēēp

2. a cow kissed mȳ _____.

   • hand   • fēēt   • nōse

1. shē has a little **f**_____.

2. hē has a **b**_____ fish.

stōry Ītems

1. did a hōrse jump the crēēk?

     ● yes   ● nō

2. the cow ran up to the ▬▬▬ of the crēēk.

     ● sīde   ● bank   ● top

then the cow jumped.

a ___ ___ ___   r ___ ___ ___

o ___ ___ ___   s ___ ___ ___

d ___ ___ ___   b ___ ___ ___

shē līked to walk. sō shē walked in
the park. shē met a girl and a dog.

1. shē līked to _____.

   • sit   • park   • walk

2. shē met a girl and a _____.

   • man   • dog   • cat

---

wē got a little rabbit.

that rabbit jumped.

1. _____ got a little rabbit.

   • you   • wē   • mē

2. that _____ jumped.

   • cow   • dog   • rabbit

1. the little b_____
   is in the can.

2. the big bug is n_____
   in the can.

stōry Ītems

1. the ▬▬▬▬ jumped ōver the crēēk.

    • hōrse   • bank   • cow

2. the cow boy gāve the cow a ▬▬▬.

    • car   • kiss   • hōrse

he kissed his cow.

d __ __ __   s __ __ __

J __ __ __   t __ __ __

b __ __ __   m __ __ __

shē was not fat. shē had a hat.

shē sat on a cat.

1. _____ was not fat.

   • mē   • sēē   • shē

2. shē sat on a _____.

   • cat   • rat   • hat

---

the cow āte fīve hot cākes.

shē did not get sick.

1. the _____ āte fīve hot cākes.

   • cow   • cat   • cāke

2. shē did not get _____.

   • fat   • sick   • sad

1. the man is n_____ little.

2. his d_____ is little.

1. māke _r_ in the circle.

2. māke _s_ in the box.

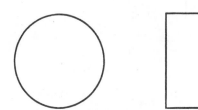

---

a girl went fishiñg. but shē did not get fish at the crēēk. shē got wet.

1. shē went ░░░░░░.

• runniñg   • walkiñg   • fishiñg

2. but shē did not get fish at ░░░░░░.

• the lāke   • hōme   • the crēēk

---

a cow had a cōld. sō the cow got a book. then the cow went to bed.

1. the cow had a ░░░░░░.

• gōld   • cōld   • hōld

2. then the cow went to ░░░░░░.

• a book   • bed   • the boy

1. the **C** _____ can jump.

2. the men are **W** _____ .

3. the **C** _____
on the cow is happy.

he was wet and cold.

a _____

b _____

c _____

d _____

e _____

f _____

1. jill's sister did not _____.

  • crȳ   • trēē   • trȳ

2. jill said, "if you trȳ, you will not

  have to ████____."

  • trȳ   • crȳ   • trēē

1. māke _t_ in the box.

2. māke _c_ in the circle.

1. hē has some **f**_____.

2. that **r**_____ is fat.

she was named jill.

_ _

_ _

the girl got a pot. then shē got a fish.
shē said, "this fish will gō in the pot."

1. the ▬▬▬▬ got a pot.

   • man   • boy   • girl

2. shē said, "this ▬▬▬▬ will gō in the pot."

   • fan   • fish   • flȳ

---

mom had lots of cars. shē had a red car.
shē had nīne whīte cars.

1. ▬▬▬▬ had lots of cars.

   • man   • men   • mom

2. shē had nīne ▬▬▬▬ cars.

   • back   • whīte   • big

k ___ ___ ___	f ___ ___ ___
u ___ ___ ___ ___	y ___ ___ ___
z ___ ___ ___	r ___ ___ ___

1. did jill trȳ to do thin͡gs?

     • yes   • nō

2. did her sister trȳ to do thin͡gs?

     • yes   • nō

3. can her sister rēad books?

     • yes   • nō

---

1. māke _r_ in the circle.

2. māke _d_ in the box.

1. they are in a l̲|̲_____.

2. the girl is gōin͡g

    after the **f**_____.

---

did her sister try?

_____

a boy *did* not talk to girls. hē talk**ed**
to cows. hē talk**ed** to gōats.

1. a boy *did* not talk to _____.

- ● gā̄tes
- ● girls
- ● cats

2. hē _____ to gōats.

- ● walk**ed**
- ● talk**ed**
- ● said

---

the rabbit went down a slīde. ꟻhē went
on her nōse. her nōse was sōre.

1. the _____ went down a slīde.

- ● ram
- ● rat
- ● rabbit

2. ꟻhē went on her _____.

- ● sock
- ● nōse
- ● rōse

p _ _ _ _	f _ _ _ _
d _ _ _ _	g _ _ _ _
b _ _ _ _	c _ _ _ _

1. Jon was gōīng to bāke a _____ cāke.
   - big   - cat   - fish

2. did his sister help him?
   - yes   - nō

3. did his mother help him?
   - yes   - nō

---

1. māke _s_ in the circle.

2. māke _r_ in the box.

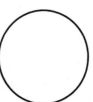

1. that **b**_____ is in the mud.

2. hē is **S**_____.

---

he baked a cake.

a dog went fishing. the dog did not get
fish. a boy got nine fish.

1. a dog went ▭.

- hunting   - shopping   - fishing

2. the dog did not get ▭.

- fat   - fish   - cold

---

a boy had a red tooth brush. hē had the
tooth brush in a box. hē had the box in
his room.

1. a boy had a red ▭ brush.

- hand   - thing   - tooth

2. hē had the box in his ▭.

- room   - moon   - hōme

a ___ ___ ___	d ___ ___ ___
b ___ ___ ___	e ___ ___ ___
c ___ ___ ___	f ___ ___ ___

1. Jon mā̄de a fish 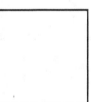.

- bā̄ke - lā̄ke - cā̄ke

2. Jon got very _____.

- big - sick - fat

---

1. mā̄ke x in the box.

2. mā̄ke r in the circle.

1. the C_____ is in a trēē.

2. the girl is n_____ in the trēē.

---

jon ate the cake.

a fat ēagle did not flȳ. the ēagle said, "I will crȳ."

her sister said, "if you trȳ, you can flȳ."

1. a fat _____ did not flȳ.

  ● flȳ   ● rat   ● ēagle

2. her sister said, "if you trȳ, you can _____."

  ● rēad   ● flȳ   ● sit

---

a little bug got mad at a dog. the dog said, "gō hōme, bug." sō the bug bit the dog.

1. a little _____ got mad at a dog.

  ● bus   ● boy   ● bug

2. sō the little bug bit the _____.

  ● boy   ● dog   ● man

J — — — —   V — — — —

i — — — —   k — — — —

W — — — —   f — — — —

1. spot did not ▬▬▬ well.
   • ēat   • ēar   • hēar

2. the man in the stōre said, "give mē a ▬▬▬."
   • lot   • dīme   • bit

3. did spot give him a dīme fōr the bōnes?
   • yes   • nō

---

1. māke _z_ in the circle.

2. māke _s_ ōver the circle.

◯

1. shē is in a **c**_____.

2. the **m**_____ is big.

---

spot did not hear.

the boy had a little ship. his ship was
on a lāke. hē had fun in that ship.

1. the ▬▬▬▬▬ had a little ship.

   ● boy   ● bus   ● toy

2. hē had ▬▬▬▬▬ in that ship.

   ● sand   ● fun   ● fish

---

a duck walked on a rōad. a man cāme up
in his car. hē said, "let mē give you a
rīde."

1. a duck ▬▬▬▬▬ on a rōad.

   ● walked   ● jumped   ● talked

2. a man said, "let mē give you a ▬▬▬▬▬.

   ● duck   ● rōad   ● rīde

c ___ ___ ___	t ___ ___ ___
k ___ ___ ___	g ___ ___ ___
v ___ ___ ___	d ___ ___ ___

1. was spot a cat?

   ● yes   ● nō

2. did spot hēar well?

   ● yes   ● nō

3. spot said to the cop, "you are a ▬▬▬ cop."

   ● fat   ● good   ● bad

---

1. māke _b_ ōver the box.

2. māke _c_ in the box.

1. the cat is on a **b**_____.

2. a **r**_____ is on the cat.

---

spot met a cop._____

sal līked to run and jump. but shē did not līke to ēat. wē said, "if you ēat, you can rēad a book."

1. _____ līked to run and jump.

   • sat   • sad   • sal

2. but shē did not līke to _____.

   • talk   • ēat   • ēar

---

a big shark went after a little fish. the shark did not get the fish. the fish swam too fast.

1. a big _____ went after a little fish.

   • cat   • hōrse   • shark

2. the fish swam too _____.

   • slōw   • fast   • fat

h ___ ___ ___	t ___ ___ ___
m ___ ___ ___	z ___ ___ ___
p ___ ___ ___	y ___ ___ ___

1. don līked to ask _____.

 • what • when • whȳ

2. don dug a hōle in the _____.

 • yard • farm • car

3. don got a can of _____ pāint.

 • what • whīte • whȳ

---

1. māke <u>x</u> in the circle.

2. māke <u>m</u> ōver the circle.

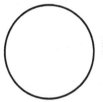

1. the girl has a **f**_____.

2. the boy has a **h**_____.

---

he dug a big hole.

sid was a fat dog. sid walked and walked. but sid did not run fast.

1. _____ was a fat dog.

- sam   • sid   • sad

2. but sid did not _____ fast.

- talk   • jump   • run

---

nell was a whīte hōrse. shē ran in the rāin. shē ran as fast as a dēēr.

1. _____ was a whīte hōrse.

- bill   • fill   • nell

2. shē _____ as fast as a dēēr.

- ran   • slid   • jumps

---

y __ __ __   c __ __ __

v __ __ __   g __ __ __

w __ __ __   f __ __ __

1. whāt did don līke to ask?

   ● whȳ   ● when   ● whĕre

2. whŏ askĕd him whăt hē was dōing with his bīke?

   ● his brother   ● his mother   ● his sister

___

1. māke _m_ in the circle.

2. māke _a_ ōver the circle.

3. māke _r_ under the circle.

___

1. māke _t_ ōver the box.

2. māke _s_ under the box.

3. māke _a_ in the box.

don painted and painted.

sam went fishing at the lāke. hē was
at the lāke fōr a little tīme. hē cāme
back with fīve fish.

1. sam went _____ at the lāke.
   - swimming   - hunting   - fishing

2. hē cāme back with _____ fish.
   - fīve   - big   - nīne

spot līked to ēat mēat.
and spot āte bōnes.
spot had a lot of bōnes.

1. _____ līked to ēat mēat.
   - pot   - spot   - stop

2. spot had a _____ of bōnes.
   - room   - tub   - lot

1. the robbers cāme from the stōre with ‗‗‗‗‗.

  • bags of toys   • bags of monēy

  • bags of dīmes

2. the robbers had a big ‗‗‗‗.

  • ēar   • bag   • hōrn

3. spot bit the robbers on the ‗‗‗‗.

  • legs   • ēars   • nōse

4. was the cop happy?

  • yes   • nō

---

1. māke t in the circle.

2. māke s ōver the box.

3. māke m in the box.

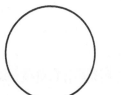

---

1. māke 4 under the box.

2. māke b in the box.

3. māke o ōver the box.

spot bit the robbers.

a cow was sleeping in the barn. a bug
went to sleep on the cow. the bug
said, "this cow is a good bed."

1. a cow was sleeping in the ▭▭▭▭.
   ● lāke   ● barn   ● yard

2. did the bug līke to sleep on the cow? ▭▭▭▭
   ● yes   ● nō

---

the car ran into a trēē. the trēē
fell on a barn. the hōrse in the
barn got mad.

1. what did the car run into? ▭▭▭▭
   ● a car   ● a trēē   ● a hōrse

2. the ▭▭▭▭ got mad.
   ● hōrse   ● cow   ● car

1. the little bird said, "I am crȳing bēcause
   I can not ▭▭▭▭."
   - talk   - flȳ   - walk

2. his sisters said, "wē will tēach you to flȳ
   if you stop ▭▭▭▭."
   - trȳing   - flȳing   - crȳing

3. does the little bird līke to flȳ now?
   - yes   - nō

---

1. māke r ōver the circle.

2. māke t in the box.

3. māke s in the circle.

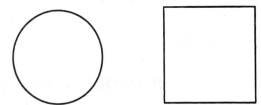

---

1. māke a circle under the box.

2. māke t ōver the box.

3. māke h in the box.

an eagle was crying.

a girl loved rocks. the other dāy shē
got fīve rocks. now shē has a big
pīle of rocks.

1. whot did the girl love? ▭▭▭▭
   ● socks   ● logs   ● rocks

2. now shē has a big ▭▭▭▭ of rocks.
   ● bag   ● pīle   ● room

a man had an ōld car that did not
start. hē gāve it a kiss. then the
ōld car started.

1. a man had an ōld ▭▭▭▭.
   ● car   ● bug   ● can

2. hē gāve it a ▭▭▭▭.
   ● lick   ● kick   ● kiss

1. the farmer had his best buttons on his .

   • hat   • socks   • pants

2. a man cāme to the farm to .

   • sēē buttons   • sell buttons

   • buȳ buttons

3. did the farmer sell some of his buttons?

   • yes   • no

---

1. māke __i__ in the box.

2. māke __c__ under the box.

3. māke __b__ ōver the circle.

---

1. māke __r__ in the circle.

2. māke a box ōver the circle.

3. māke __6__ under the circle.

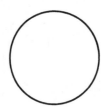

that farmer had buttons.

jill went fishing and got fīve fish.

she ran awāy when a fox cāme nēar.

the fox āte her fish.

1. jill went _____.

 • digging   • swimming   • fishing

2. the _____ āte her fish.

 • box   • fox   • for

mother gāve pam some gōld. when pam cāme
back, she said, "I sōld the gōld so that I can
get a bīke." now pam has a red bīke.

1. what did mother give to pam? _____

 • a bīke   • some gōld   • a hōld

2. what did pam get? _____

 • a bīke   • some gōld   • a sack

1. the farmer sōld the buttons that held up _____.

   • his hat   • his pants   • his cōat

2. then his pants _____.

   • held up   • had buttons   • fell down

3. now the farmer has monēy, but he has no _____.

   • pants   • socks   • buttons

---

1. māke a circle next to the box.

2. māke _t_ in the circle.

3. māke _s_ in the box.

---

1. māke _e_ under the circle.

2. māke _5_ ōver the box.

3. māke _t_ in the box.

he sold his buttons.

---

her mom gāve her a kiss. so she gāve
her dog a kiss. then the dog gāve
the cat a kiss.

1. what did her mom give her? ▬▬▬▬

    ● a kick   ● a card   ● a kiss

2. the dog kissed the ▬▬▬▬.

    ● mom   ● cat   ● dog

---

a big tīger met a little tīger. the
big tīger said, "let's ēat." so the
little tīger āte the big tīger.

1. the big tīger said, "▬▬▬▬."

    ● let's ēat   ● let's go   ● let's talk

2. what did the little tīger ēat? ▬▬▬▬

    ● the little tīger   ● the big tīger   ● cōrn

1. how did spot go on her trip?

     ● in a b͞oat   ● in a truck   ● in a car

2. what town was she looking for?

     ● down   ● dim   ● town

3. what did spot get in the st͞ore?

     ● a bag of toys   ● a bag of b͞ones

     ● a bag of dogs

---

1. m͞ake a box next to the circle.

2. m͞ake _r_ ͞over the circle.

3. m͞ake _v_ under the box.

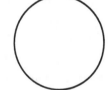

---

1. m͞ake _9_ ͞over the box.

2. m͞ake _v_ under the circle.

3. m͞ake _d_ in the box.

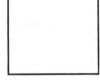

where can I get gas?

---

a boy did not crȳ. the other
boys said, "we will tēach you to
crȳ." so they did.

1. a _____ did not crȳ.

   • girl   • man   • boy

2. what did the other boys tēach the boy? _____

   • how to trȳ   • how to flȳ
   • how to crȳ

---

a bird had six hats. she gāve fīve
hats to her sisters. now the bird
has one hat.

1. the bird had _____ hats.

   • one   • six   • fīve

2. now the bird has _____ hat.

   • one   • six   • fīve

a farmer had an ōld car that did not stop. the car went into a pond. the farmer said, "this car thinks it is a fish."

1. the car did not ______.
   - stop
   - run
   - yes

2. the car went ______.
   - up a hill
   - into a pond
   - nēar the lāke

---

a boy dropped a button into the lāke. a fish looked at the button. "mȳ, that is a fīne thing," the fish said. so the fish took the button to his hōme.

1. a ______ dropped a button.
   - button
   - thing
   - boy

2. a ______ looked at the button.
   - fish
   - fin
   - girl

3. the fish took the button ______.
   - on his fin
   - to his mother
   - to his hōme

---

will she stay at home?

____

a girl had thrēē red socks. she said, "I dōn't nēēd thrēē socks." so she gāve a sock to her cat. the cat has a sock on his tāil.

1. a girl had thrēē ______.
   - red hats
   - red dogs
   - red socks
2. she gāve a sock to her ______.
   - cat
   - can
   - mom
3. the cat has a sock ______.
   - in his māil
   - on his nōse
   - on his tāil

---

1. māke a box ōver the circle.
2. māke b in the box.
3. māke c under the circle.

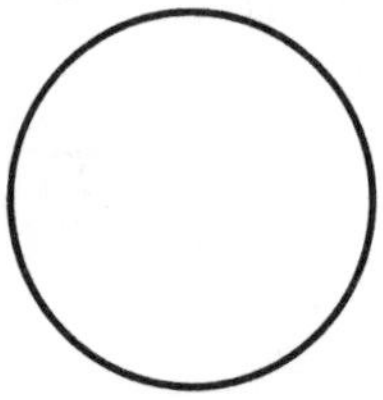

---

1. māke 4 ōver the box.
2. māke m ōver the 4.
3. māke 6 in the circle.

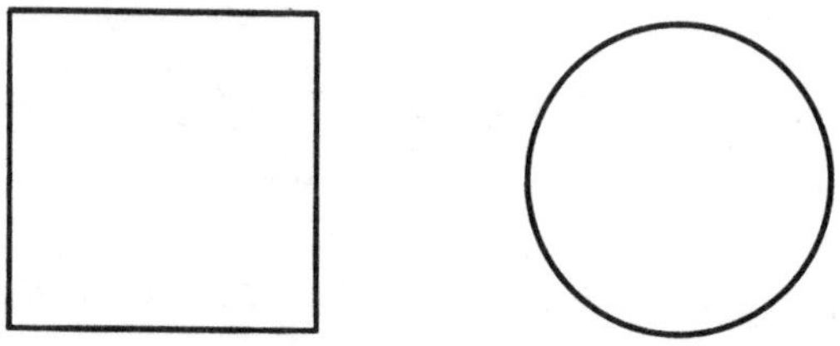

1. whāt did this dog līke to do?

- walk, walk, walk
- tāke, tāke, tāke
- talk, talk, talk

2. did the dog līke to plāy ball?

- yes
- no

3. so the man got very ▆▆▆▆___.

- mad
- sad
- ōld

---

1. māke a circle next to the box.

2. māke _a_ under the box.

3. māke _e_ in the circle.

---

1. māke _g_ in the circle.

2. māke _n_ ōver the circle.

3. māke _o_ under the box.

a boy loved to rīde cows. his dad said,
"whȳ do you rīde a cow when you have a
hōrse?"

so now the hōrse rīdes the cow.

1. what did the boy love to rīde? ▬▬▬▬
   - ● dogs
   - ● cows
   - ● hōrses

2. a ▬▬▬▬ rīdes the cow now.
   - ● hōrse
   - ● boy
   - ● cow

---

a girl had nīne buttons on her hat. her mom
gāve her another button. now the girl has
ten buttons on her hat.

1. what did her mom give her? ▬▬▬▬
   - ● nīne buttons
   - ● another button
   - ● ten buttons

2. she has ▬▬▬▬ buttons now.
   - ● nīne
   - ● one
   - ● ten

she can read, read, read.

1. the small bug did not have a ▭▭▭▭▭.

     • sister   • hōme   • hōle

2. where did he trȳ to live?

     • in a cup   • in a shack   • in a stall

3. at last he cāme to a ▭▭▭▭▭.

     • ball   • town   • man

4. did the bug līke the ball?

     • yes   • no

---

1. māke a box ōver the circle.

2. māke _d_ ōver the box.

3. māke _m_ under the circle.

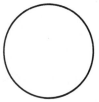

---

1. māke a _6_ in the circle.

2. māke a _3_ under the box.

3. māke _h_ ōver the box.

a man cāme to the farm. he said,

"I want to buȳ some cows."

so the farmer sōld him six cows.

1. what did the man want? ▬▬▬
- • farms   • men   • cows

2. the farmer sōld ▬▬▬ cows.
- • six   • fīve   • no

---

a girl got mad at her dog for digging

hōles. her dog dug up gōld.

now the girl is not mad.

1. her dog ▬▬▬ up gōld.
- • dug   • man   • bug

2. the girl is not ▬▬▬ now.
- • had   • mud   • mad

he went into the ball.

1. the bug went to slēēp in the _____.

    ● hall   ● ball   ● bed

2. when he wōke up, the ball was _____.

    ● runnĩng   ● rōllĩng   ● walkĩng

3. what did the girl sāy to the bug?

    ● "I love bugs."   ● "I ēat bugs."

    ● "I hāte bugs."

---

1. māke a circle ōver the box.

2. māke _u_ under the box.

3. māke _s_ ōver the circle.

---

1. māke _k_ under the circle.

2. māke _s_ ōver the box.

3. māke a _2_ in the circle.

a farmer was mad at a bug. "stop ēatiñg mȳ
cōrn," the farmer said. so the bug stoppe**d**
ēatiñg cōrn and āte the farmer's hat.

1. a ▬▬▬▬ was mad.
   • bug   • farmer   • girl

2. the farmer said, "stop ēatiñg mȳ ▬▬▬▬."
   • farm   • hat   • cōrn

---

an ēagle fell from a trēē.
he fell on a dog.
the dog started to crȳ.

1. an ēagle fell on a ▬▬▬▬.
   • dog   • trēē   • ēagle

2. what did the dog start to do? ▬▬▬▬
   • crȳ   • run   • bark

this ball is my home.

1. the small bug wanted to ______ in the ball.

- look
- stāy
- run

2. the bug said, "I will ______ with you."

- plāy
- stāy
- sit

3. did the girl want to come to the party?

- yes
- no

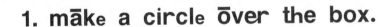

1. māke a circle ōver the box.

2. māke s in the box.

3. māke r ōver the circle.

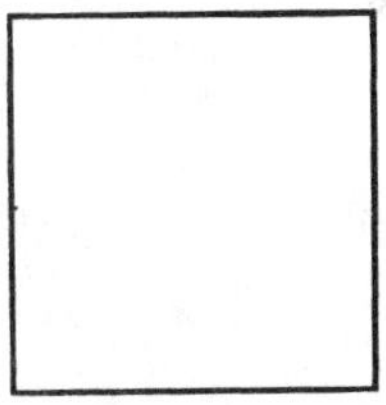

---

1. māke he in the box.

2. māke b under the circle.

3. māke a 7 ōver the box.

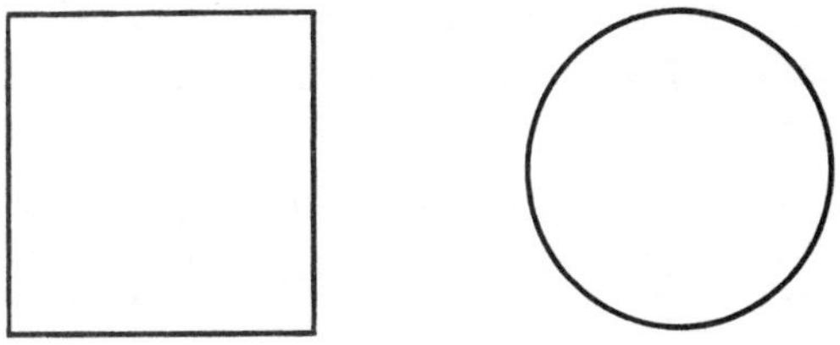

a shark met a cat. the shark said, "get on
mȳ back and go for a rīde." so the cat got
on the shark's back and went for a rīde.

1. the cat got on the shark's _____.

   ● nōse   ● back   ● fin

2. where did the cat go? _____

   ● for a rīde   ● for a cop   ● for a shark

---

a boy asked spot, "whȳ is your nōse cōld?"
spot said, "so you can fēēl it when I kiss
you." then she gāve the boy a kiss.

1. spot had a cōld _____.

   ● tāil   ● nōse   ● ēar

2. what did she give the boy? _____

   ● a nōse   ● a cōld   ● a kiss

---

please let me stay.

1. a tall girl wanted the bug to fīnd .

- a hōrse   • another hōme

- another barn

2. her  cāme into the room.

- brother   • sister   • mother

3. the girl māde a _____ with her brother.

- bad   • wish   • bet

---

1. māke a box next to the circle.

2. māke _m_ in the box.

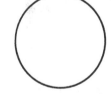

3. māke _r_ ōver the circle.

---

1. māke an _8_ under the box.

2. māke _y_ ōver the box.

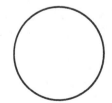

3. māke _p_ in the circle.

a man was gōīng on a trip. there was
room in his car for a bīke and a dog.
but then there was no room for the man.

1. the man was gōīng on a _____.

    ● bīke   ● dog   ● trip

2. there was no room for the _____.

    ● man   ● dog   ● car

---

ron asked a fish, "what do you līke
to ēat?" the fish said, "I love bugs."
so ron gāve the fish a big bug.

1. what did the fish līke to ēat? _____

    ● cats   ● fish   ● bugs

2. what did ron give the fish? _____

    ● a big bar   ● a big bug   ● a little bug

I will take that bet.

1. did the brother sēē the bug in the ball?

    ● yes   ● no

2. whȳ did the ball start to rōll?

    ● the bug crīed.   ● the brother bet.

    ● the bug ran.

3. how did the stōry end?

    ● the bug stopped.   ● the bug stāyed.

    ● the bug went far.

---

1. māke a box under the circle.

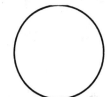

2. māke _t_ under the box.

3. māke _b_ under the t.

1. māke a _4_ in the box.

2. māke _c_ in the circle.

3. māke _t_ ōver the circle.

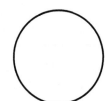

fīve dogs dug a hōle to look for bōnes.

they saw gōld in the hōle.

dogs cannot ēat gōld, so the dogs got mad.

1. fīve dogs dug a ▬▬▬▬.

   ● bōnes   ● hōle   ● gōld

2. what can't dogs ēat? ▬▬▬▬

   ● gōld   ● mēat   ● ham

---

there was a cat that loved to ēat, ēat, ēat.

so she sat on her sēat, sēat, sēat. and she

āte lots of mēat, mēat, mēat.

1. what did the cat love to do? ▬▬▬▬

   ● hit   ● ēat   ● mēat

2. what did she ēat? ▬▬▬▬

   ● mēat   ● ēat   ● bēans

make that ball roll.

1. a small elephant alwāys ▃▃▃▃.

     • jumped down   • sat down   • fell down

2. the elephant said, "I ▃▃▃▃ to fall."

     • līke   • hāte   • want

3. a tall girl gāve him ▃▃▃▃.

     • some fish   • some grass
     • some glasses

4. was the elephant happy at the end of the stōry?

     • yes   • no

---

1. māke a circle ōver the box.

2. māke _g_ ōver the circle.

3. māke _s_ ōver the _g_ .

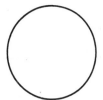

---

1. māke _y_ under the circle.

2. māke a _9_ under the box.

3. māke _a_ ōver the box.

spot had a dīme. the man at the stōre said,
"you can get some bōnes for that dīme."
spot said, "no, I want some ham."

1. spot had a ▭.

  • dīme   • bōne   • stōre

2. what did spot want? ▭

  • some bōnes   • some ham   • some dīmes

---

sam māde a mud cāke.
he āte the cāke bȳ him self.
the cāke māde him sick.

1. what did sam māke? ▭

  • a mud lāke   • a fish cāke   • a mud cāke

2. he āte the cāke ▭.

  • bȳ him self   • in his room   • in the yard

do you need glasses?

1. the dog ▬▬▬ to rēad books.

  • hāted   • loved   • trīed

2. what was the tall man looking for?

  • his hat   • his ball   • his book

3. whȳ was the tall man mad at the dog?

  • the dog took his book.

  • the dog took his ball.

  • the dog took his hat.

4. the dog hid the book when the tall man was ▬▬▬.

  • in the room   • in the hall   • slēēping

---

1. māke the word <u>sun</u> in the circle.

2. māke the word <u>cat</u> under the circle.

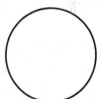

---

1. māke a box next to the circle.

2. māke <u>r</u> in the box.

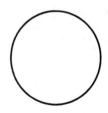

3. māke <u>b</u> under the circle.

pam had ten footballs. she gāve her sister
one football. now pam has nīne footballs.

1. what did pam have? ▬▬▬▬
   - ten sisters   ● one football
   - ten footballs

2. how many footballs did she give to her sister? ▬▬▬▬
   - six   ● seven   ● one

---

a small cat had a ham. a big cat said, "give
me a bīte." so the small cat bit the big cat.

1. what did the small cat have? ▬▬▬▬
   - a ham   ● a hat   ● a home

2. the big cat said, "▬▬▬▬."
   - give me a bit   ● give me a bīte
   - give me a ham

will you play ball?

1. did walter plāy football well?

    ● yes   ● no

2. when walter ran to get a pass, he _____.

    ● kickₑd the football   ● droppₑd the football

    ● held the football

3. the other boys tōld him, "you _____ drop the football."

    ● also   ● never   ● alwāys

4. walter was a very _____ boy.

    ● sad   ● mēan   ● glad

---

1. mākₑ the word <u>log</u> under the circlₑ.

2. mākₑ the word <u>fat</u> in the box.

---

1. mākₑ <u>p</u> ōver the box.

2. mākₑ <u>J</u> ōver the <u>p</u>.

3. mākₑ <u>h</u> under the box.

a bird said, "I cannot flȳ."
the bird's brother said, "I will shōw you
how to flȳ." so the bird and his brother
went to an ēagle.

1. a bird said, "_____."

- I will not flȳ
- I cannot flȳ
- you do not trȳ

2. where did the bird and his brother go?

- to a farm
- to a rabbit
- to an ēagle

---

a girl had six cows. she gāve thrēē cows to
her dad. now the girl has thrēē cows.

1. how many cows did the girl give to her dad?

- one
- six
- thrēē

2. how many cows does she have now?

- one
- thrēē
- six

why do you always fall?

Name ______________________

1. there was a big football [redacted].
   - nāme
   - gāme
   - plāy

2. where was the gāme plāyed?
   - in a lot
   - in a stōre
   - in a room

3. was walter plāying on his tēam?
   - yes
   - no

4. walter said, "that other tēam is gōing to [redacted]."
   - wish
   - walk
   - win

5. walter said, "I [redacted] I could help mȳ tēam."
   - walk
   - wish
   - went

---

1. māke __h__ next to the box.

2. māke __k__ ōver the box.

3. māke __f__ ōver the __h__.

---

1. māke the word __it__ under the box.

2. māke the word __so__ ōver the circle.

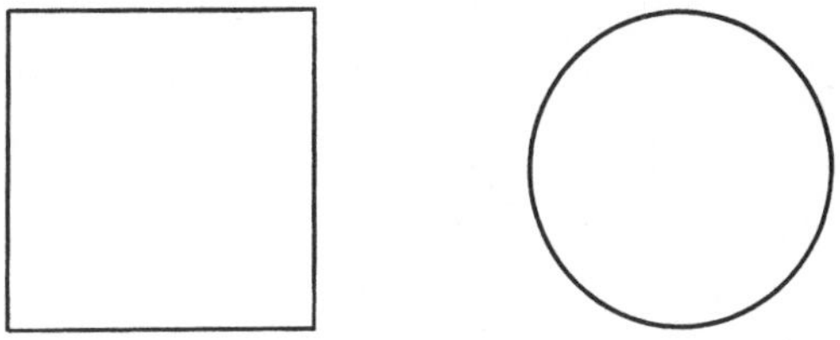

fīve men took gōld from a stōre. a cop
stoppєd them. now the men havє no gōld.

1. wherє did the men get the gōld?

   ● from a cop   ● from a jāil   ● from a stōre

2. what do the men havє now?

   ● a cop   ● no gōld   ● some gōld

---

jill's sister said, "I cannot rēad. but I will
trȳ." the next dāy, she said, "I cannot rēad.
but I will trȳ." she kept tryiñg and now she
is rēadiñg.

1. what did jill's sister sāy?

   ● I will trȳ.   ● I will crȳ.   ● I will flȳ.

2. what can jill's sister do now?

   ● crȳ   ● rēad   ● rōad

how could they win?

Name ______________________ WORKSHEET **138** SIDE 1

1. the other tēam had two ______.

   - balls
   - boys
   - scōres

2. the ______ plāyer on walter's tēam cut his arm.

   - big
   - best
   - tall

3. did the tēam ask walter to plāy?

   - yes
   - no

4. whȳ did they ask walter?

   - they nēēded a ball.
   - they nēēded a plāy.
   - they nēēded a plāyer.

---

1. māke __b__ next to the circle.
2. māke __t__ under the circle.
3. māke __s__ under the __b__ .

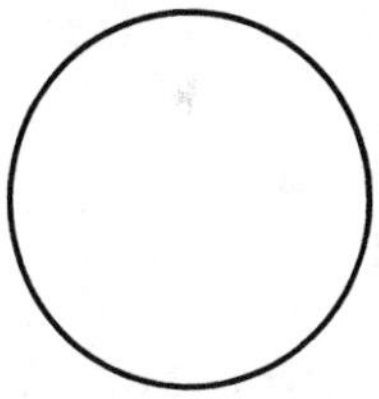

---

1. māke the word mad in the box.
2. māke the word sad in the circle.

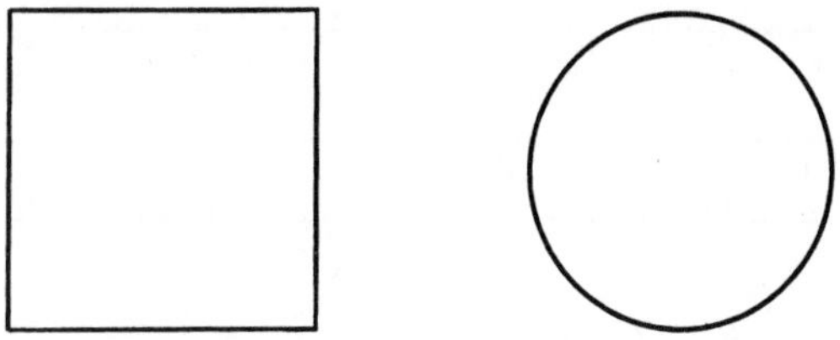

jāne said, "I can plāy football better than any boy."

the boys said, "hō, hō." but jāne was the best plāyer in the gāme.

1. what did the boys sāy?

- "oh, no"   - "no, no"   - "hō, hō"

2. did jāne plāy well?

- yes   - no

---

the talking dog said, "I will go in the hall, hall, hall." so he went to the hall. then he said, "I will plāy some ball, ball, ball." so he did.

1. where did the dog go?

- to a ball   - to the hall   - to a wall

2. what did he do?

- plāyed ball   - called   - āte salt

"come here," they called.

1. walter's tēam was gōin͠g to _____.

    ● kick the ball   ● pass the ball   ● run the ball

2. did the other boys think that they could kick the ball that far?

    ● yes   ● no

3. walter said, "I _____ I could kick the ball that far."

    ● thank   ● think   ● plāyer

4. walter said to himself, "I will not _____."

    ● fall   ● kick   ● run

---

1. māke _b_ ōver the box.

2. māke _r_ next to the _b_ .

3. māke _s_ ōver the _b_ .

---

1. māke the word <u>fox</u> under the circle.

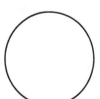

2. māke the word <u>flȳ</u> in the box.

jāne did not līke fish. so she gāve her fish to her dog. the dog said, "it is fun to ēat fish."

1. what didn't jāne līke?

   ● dogs   ● fish   ● cāke

2. what did she do with her fish?

   ● gāve it to her dog   ● āte it   ● sat on it

---

thrēē bugs wanted to plāy football. the football was a sēēd. they had a good gāme. but one bug āte the sēēd. then the bugs had to stop plāyiñg football.

1. how many bugs plāyed football?

   ● thrēē   ● one   ● six

2. where is the sēēd?

   ● one bug cooked it.   ● one bug āte it.

   ● thrēē bugs āte it.

I will not fall.

1. what did walter do in this story?

  ● ran with the ball   ● picked up the ball

  ● kicked the ball

2. the ball went līke a ▬▬▬▬.

  ● stop   ● shop   ● shot

3. they called, "that's the wāy to ▬▬▬▬."

  ● run   ● kick   ● shot

4. what did walter's tēam nēed to win?

  ● one mōre scōre   ● one mōre boy

  ● one mōre ball

_____

1. māke _s_ next to the circle.

2. māke _t_ ōver the _s_ .

3. māke _y_ under the _s_ .

_____

1. māke the word _fun_ ōver the box.

2. māke the word _box_ under the circle.

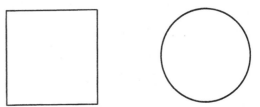

jan got in a tall trēē. her mom said, "dōn't fall from that tall trēē." jan did not fall from the trēē. she jumpₑd from the trēē.

1. whereₑ did jan go?

● in a tall trēē   ● in a hall   ● nēₐr a ball

2. how did jan get from the tall trēē?

● she fell.   ● she jumpₑd.   ● she ran.

a farmer got on a hōrsₑ. the hōrsₑ did not want to go. she wanted to ēₐt. so the farmer gāvₑ the hōrsₑ some sēēds. she atₑ the sēēds. then she and the farmer took a rīdₑ.

1. what did the farmer give the hōrsₑ?

● some wēēds   ● some kicks   ● some sēēds

2. what did the hōrsₑ and the farmer do?

● they took a rīdₑ.   ● they startₑd to crȳ.

he can kick the ball.

1. walter said, "I think I can _____ the ball all the wāy."

      ● run   ● kick   ● jump

2. did walter's tēam win the gāme?

      ● yes   ● no

3. whȳ was walter happy?

      ● bēcause he āte candy

      ● bēcause he was the star of the gāme

      ● bēcause he hit the ball

4. can walter plāy football any tīme he wants?

      ● yes   ● no

---

1. māke a box ōver the circle.

2. māke _t_ in the box.

3. māke _n_ under the circle.

---

1. māke the word car in the box.

2. māke the word ōld under the box.

a cow did not go "moo." that cow went
"arf, arf."
every tīme the cow went "arf, arf," the
farmer said, "I think I hēar a dog."

1. what did the cow sāy?

● "arf, arf"   ● "moo"   ● "boo, hoo"

2. the farmer said, "I think I hēar a ▆▆▆▆▆."

● cow   ● dog   ● cat

dan's mom said, "if you ēat lots of mēat,
you will get tall." so dan āte and āte. but he
did not get tall. he got fat.

1. what did his mom tell him to ēat?

● gōats   ● mēat   ● cōrn

2. what did dan get?

● mēat   ● tall   ● fat

walter was happy.

Jāne said, "I will kick the ball far."
tim said, "I will hōld the ball for you."
Jāne kicked the ball. she kicked the ball
very far.

1. what did Jāne want to kick? _____
   ● the ball   ● the boy   ● the bōat

2. what did tim hōld? _____
   ● the bōat   ● the boy   ● the ball

3. what did Jāne kick? _____
   ● the toy   ● the boy   ● the ball

_____

a girl went out for the running tēam.
the boys on the tēam said, "that girl thinks
she can run fast."
the girl ran faster than the boys. then she
said, "hō, hō."

1. the girl went out for the running _____.
   ● nōse   ● fast   ● tēam

2. did the boys think she could run fast? _____
   ● yes   ● no

3. who ran faster? _____
   ● the boys   ● the girl   ● the tēam

4. what did the girl sāy after she ran? _____
   ● "he, he"   ● "ha, ha"   ● "hō, hō"

rēad this sentence.

the dog was fat.

1. circle the word <u>was</u>.

2. māke a līne ōver the word <u>the</u>.

---

rēad this sentence.

a fish āte a ball.

1. māke a līne ōver the word <u>fish</u>.

2. circle the word <u>ball</u>.

---

rēad this sentence.

a girl had a red hat.

1. māke a līne ōver the word <u>red</u>.

2. circle the word <u>girl</u>.

1. what is the nāme of the cow in this stōry?

_____

   ● walter   ● moo   ● carmen

2. carmen has a very _____ moo.

   ● loud   ● little   ● fast

3. where did the children go? _____

   ● to the stōre   ● to the farm   ● to the lot

4. they cāme to _____ cows.

   ● see   ● pet   ● hit

5. one chīld fell _____.

   ● in a box   ● in a hōle   ● in a crēēk

> thrēē men sat in a car.

1. circle the word <u>car</u>.

2. māke a līne ōver the word <u>men</u>.

> her nāme was nell.

1. māke a līne under the word <u>her</u>.

2. māke a līne ōver the word <u>nell</u>.

a little shark was trȳing to swim. a fish
cāme up and askₑd, "can I givₑ you a hand?"
the shark said, "fish dōn't have hands.
they have fins."

1. the fish askₑd if he could givₑ the

shark a _____. ● hand ● trick ● fish

2. do fish have hands? _____ ● yes ● no

six old men and one dog went to the
lāke. fīvₑ men said, "we hātₑ to swim." so
they sat on the shōrₑ.

the other old man said, "I love to swim."
so he went swimmiñg. the dog went to slēēp.

1. how many men hāted to swim? _____
● six ● one ● fīvₑ

2. what did the dog do? _____
● went swimmiñg ● went to slēēp
● went to a shōw

they came to pet cows.

1. carmen had a ⎯⎯⎯⎯⎯⎯⎯⎯ moo.

   ● lēad   ● lōad   ● loud   ● little

2. carmen sāved the ⎯⎯⎯⎯⎯⎯⎯⎯ who
   fell into the hōle.

   ● cow   ● girl   ● tēacher   ● boy

3. the little girl ⎯⎯⎯⎯⎯⎯⎯⎯ the cow.

   ● kicked   ● licked   ● hit   ● kissed

4. carmen was happy bēcause she had a big,
   loud ⎯⎯⎯⎯⎯⎯⎯⎯.

   ● cow   ● moon   ● mom   ● moo

---

are you sad?

1. māke a līne ōver the word <u>sad</u>.

2. circle the word <u>are</u>.

a farmer had a cow that could not
moo. his dog said, "I will tēach that cow
to moo." so he bēgan to tēach the cow. now
the cow does not moo. she barks līke
a dog.

1. the cow could not _____.

2. who said, "I will tēach that cow to moo"?

   _____

3. what does the cow do now?

   _____

   ● moos   ● barks līke a shark
   ● swims līke a dog   ● barks līke a dog

---

1. māke __h__ in the circle.

2. māke the word <u>sat</u> under the circle.

3. māke a __9__ next to the word <u>sat</u>.

1. what did jill have in the box? _____
   - a house   - a rat   - a mouse
   - three rats

2. who did she show the mouse to? her _____
   - mother   - brother   - sister   - mouse

3. her mother said, "you can't keep that mouse in

   this _____."
   - box   - yard   - house   - room

4. where did jill take the mouse?

   to _____
   - her room   - the store   - the house
   - the yard

5. who didn't like the mouse? _____
   - because   - her mother   - in the yard
   - she was happy.

> she was not fat.

1. circle the word fat.

2. make a line over the word she.

a mouse was very sad. that mouse said,
"I will feel better if I eat a lot."

so the mouse ate and ate. at last, the
mouse was so fat that he could not leave
his house. then he said, "I am really a sad
mouse now."

1. the mouse was very _____.

2. so what did the mouse do? _____
   - ate a lot
   - sat a lot
   - went to sleep
   - went to his house

3. did the mouse feel better when he was fat? _____

4. who said, "I am really a sad mouse now"?

_____

_____

1. make a <u>2</u> over the box.

2. make the word <u>ant</u> in the box.

3. make the word <u>pig</u> over the <u>2</u>.

1. where did the little girl live?

_____

- on a tall hill
- in a barn
- in the clouds
- near a tall mountain

2. what did the girl want to see?

_____

- the top of the mountain
- because it was tall
- her mother
- the top of the clouds

3. who went with the girl up the side of the

mountain? _____

- to see the top
- her hound
- her mother
- the mountain

4. the side of the mountain was very _____.

- tall
- small
- steep
- street

---

the dog sat near the road.

1. make a line over the word road.

2. make a line under the word near.

3. circle the word sat.

a man said, "I nēēd a button for mȳ cōat." so the man went to a stōre. but he did not go to a button stōre. he went to a sēēd stōre. now he has a cōat with a big sēēd on it.

1. who said, "I nēēd a button for mȳ cōat"? _____

2. did the man go to a button stōre? _____

3. what did he buȳ at the stōre? _____

4. where is the sēēd? _____
    ● on his hat   ● in his mouth
    ● on his cōat   ● on his house

---

1. māke the word <u>no</u> ōver the circle.

2. māke <u>v</u> in the box.

3. māke the word <u>if</u> under the circle.

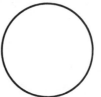
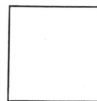

1. where did the girl live? _____

    ● nēar a lāke   ● nēar a house

    ● nēar the mountain   ● on the mountain

2. who tōld her not to go up the mountain?

_____

    ● her hound   ● bēcause it was tall

    ● her mother   ● her father

3. what did the girl see when she cāme out of

the clouds? _____

    ● a funny house   ● her father

    ● her mother   ● a loud sound

4. what did the girl hēar?

_____

    ● a house   ● her mother

    ● a loud sound   ● a hound

> she ran very fast.

1. circle the word she.

2. māke a līne under the word fast.

3. māke a līne ōver the word very.

a girl picked up a pouch. her dad
asked her, "what is in that pouch?"
the girl said, "an ouch."
her dad said, "you are silly. let me see
what is in that pouch."
he took the pouch and put his hand
inside. "ouch," he said. the girl had a fish
hook in her pouch.

1. who had an ouch pouch? _____

2. who wanted to see what was in the pouch? _____

3. what māde her dad sāy "ouch"?

_____

- • a fish fin • a hound
- • a fish hook • a hooked fish

4. did her dad get an ouch from the pouch? _____

---

1. māke a _7_ in the circle.

2. māke a _6_ ōver the circle.

3. māke _a_ next to the _6_.

1. what did the girl hēar coming from the house?

_____

- a hound   ● a mouse
- a loud house   ● a loud sound

2. who did the girl see insīde the house?

_____

- nōbody   ● her father   ● a dōor   ● a hound

3. what did the dōor do after the girl was insīde?

_____

- ōpened   ● slammed bēhīnd her
- in the house   ● brōke

4. what was hanging on the wall? a _____
- pooch   ● hound   ● couch   ● pouch

> she was not sad.

1. māke a box around the word <u>sad</u>.

2. circle the word <u>was</u>.

3. māke a līne ōver the word <u>she</u>.

a cow was rīdiñg in a car. the car ran out of gas. the cow askₑd a man, "can you givₑ me some gas?"

the man said, "I'll givₑ you gas if you givₑ me milk." now the car has gas and the man has milk.

1. the _____ was rīdiñg in a car.
   ● man   ● cow   ● dog

2. the cow askₑd a man,

"can you givₑ me _____?"
   ● some monēy   ● some milk   ● some gas

3. the man wanted the cow to givₑ him some _____.
   ● gas   ● milk   ● cākₑs

1. mākₑ the word <u>bed</u> in the circle.

2. mākₑ the word <u>men</u> under the circle.

3. mākₑ a <u>4</u> under the word <u>men</u>.

1. why didn't the girl leave the house?

   the _____.
   - door was little   ● door did not open
   - pouch was little

2. the girl asked, "is there some thing in that _____?"
   - pouch   ● door   ● yard   ● hound

3. who lived in the pouch? _____
   - a thousand years   ● the girl
   - an elf   ● an oaf

4. how many years had he lived in the pouch?

   _____

   - the elf   ● a thousand years
   - five years   ● no years

5. the elf said, "if you let me out,

   I will give you _____."
   - a hound   ● the house
   - a cloud   ● the pouch

> the dog sat on her bed.

1. circle the word <u>on</u>.

2. make a line over the word <u>dog</u>.

3. make a box around the word <u>sat</u>.

jack had a hound. jack said, "we must māke a house for this hound." so jack got some logs and some rōpe and some rocks. now the hound has a house. jack līkes the hound house so much that he gōes in there to slēēp with his hound.

1. who had a hound? _____

2. who māde the hound house? _____

3. jack māde the house of logs and rōpe and _____.

4. what does jack do in the hound house?

_____

- sits with his mouse
- slēēps with his hound
- talks in the house

1. māke a circle under the circle.

2. māke a box ōver the box.

3. cross out the circles.

1. what was hanging on the wall insĪde the house?

   a _____
   - hound   - trēē   - pouch   - pooch

2. what was insĪde that pouch? _____
   - a house   - an elf   - a hound   - an ēēl

3. what did the girl's dog sāy when the elf ran around

   the room? "_____"
   - who   - now   - owwwww   - grrrr

4. what did the elf give the girl? _____
   - when he cāme out of the pouch
   - the pouch   - a kiss

5. he tōld her, "when you are good, the pouch

   will be _____."
   - fat   - bad   - sick   - good

```
why are you crying?
```

1. māke a circle ōver the word whȳ.

2. māke a box ōver the word you.

3. māke a līne under the word are.

a bug and a dog sat bȳ the sīde of the rōad. the bug said, "I do not līke to walk. how can I get to the lāke?"

the dog said, "hop on mȳ back. I will tāke you to the lāke." so the dog took the bug to the lāke.

1. who sat bȳ the sīde of the rōad?

a _____ and a _____

2. did the bug līke to walk? _____

3. where did the bug want to go?

_____

● to the ship   ● to the log   ● to the lāke

4. who took the bug to the lāke? _____

_____

1. māke a _b_ ōver the box.

2. māke the word _ōver_ under the box.

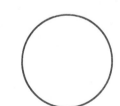

3. māke the word _under_ ōver the circle.

1. the elf tōld the girl, "when you are good,

   the pouch will be _____."

2. "when you are bad, the _____ will be _____."

3. what did the girl fīnd in the pouch? _____
   - a sock   - good   - gōld   - a gōat

4. whȳ was the pouch good to her?

   _____
   - after she was bad   - bēcause he was bad
   - bēcause she was good

5. the girl shouted, "I'm _____."
   - sick   - fat   - gōld   - rich

6. the girl and her hound started

   down the _____.
   - house   - pouch   - mountain   - clouds

7. when they rēached the bottom of the mountain,

   it was _____.
   - hot   - sun   - cōld   - lāte

8. the girl tōld her mother that she

   went _____.
   - to slēep   - to līe
   - up the mountain   - to the stōre

we want to ēat fish cāke.

1. māke a circle ōver the word <u>want</u>.

2. māke a box under the word <u>want</u>.

3. māke a līne under the word <u>fish</u>.

---

pat said, "I want to go to the moon."

sal said, "moon girls have red hats. so I will māke you a red hat." sal got a can of red pāint and māde pat a red hat. sal said, "now you can go to the moon."

1. who wanted to go to the moon? _____
   ● sal   ● the moon girls   ● pat

2. sal said, "moon girls have red _____."

3. who māde the red hat? _____

4. now can pat go to the moon? _____

---

1. māke the word <u>under</u> under the box.

2. māke the word <u>ōver</u> under the circle.

 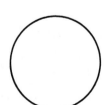

3. cross out the box.

1. the girl tōld her mother that she went _____.
   ● to slēēp   ● up the mountain   ● to the stōre

2. the elf said, "when you are good, the _____

   will be _____."

3. is it good or bad to tell a līe? _____
   ● good   ● bad

4. where did she sāy she found the pouch?

   _____

   ● bēcause she was slēēpiñg   ● on the ground
   ● in a house   ● nēar a stōre

5. what did she take from the pouch?

   _____

   ● yellōw mud   ● good   ● a hound
   ● a pouch

┌────────────────────────────────────┐
│   │
│   she found an ōld hound.   │
│   │
└────────────────────────────────────┘

1. make a box around the word <u>she</u>.

2. make a circle under the word <u>an</u>.

3. make a t ōver the word <u>hound</u>.

an elf tōld tim, "every time you tell a līe, your fēēt will get bigger."

bȳ the end of the dāy, tim had tōld so many līes that his fēēt werₑ as big as elephants. tim crīed. he tōld the elf that he would never līe again. so the elf made his fēēt small again.

1. who tōld tim that his fēēt would get bigger?

   _____

2. did tim tell many līes? _____

3. whȳ did tim's fēēt get as big as elephants?

   _____

4. who made his fēēt small again? _____

---

1. make the word <u>bad</u> in the circlₑ.

2. make the word <u>bad</u> ōver the circlₑ.

3. make the word <u>dab</u> under the circlₑ.

1. what did the girl have on her hands? _____

      ● gōld   ● mud   ● a pouch   ● an elf

2. the elf said, "when you are _____,

the _____ will be _____ to you. but

when you are _____, the _____ will

be _____ to you."

3. the girl tōld _____ līes.

      ● six   ● one   ● lots of   ● two

4. the girl tōld her mother

that _____.

      ● an elf gave her the elf
      ● an elf gave her the pouch
      ● a pooch gave her the pouch

5. how many gōld rocks were in the pouch

now? _____

      ● a thousand   ● ten   ● none   ● six

6. the girl said to herself, "I will kēēp on

doiñg _____."

      ● lots of thiñgs   ● bad thiñgs
      ● gōld thiñgs   ● good thiñgs

where did they go?

1. make m ōver the word go.

2. make a box around the word where.

3. make a circle ōver the word where.

---

one dāy a girl did something that was very good. she rēached into the magic pouch and found a mouse. this mouse was gōld. and when it walked, it went "ding, ding, ding." thrēē men wanted to buȳ the mouse, but the girl did not sell it. she kept the gōld mouse.

1. was the pouch good to the girl? _____

2. what was in the pouch? _____

3. could the mouse walk? _____

4. who kept the gōld mouse? _____

---

1. make the word ōver under the circle.

2. make the word ōver ōver the box.

3. make r in the circle.

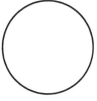 

1. an elephant wanted to sit in the _____.

    ● sit   ● lake   ● sun   ● walk

2. who was sitting in the elephant's spot? a _____

    ● fun   ● fan   ● fat   ● flȳ

3. the flȳ said, "I'll _____."

    ● fix food   ● go home

    ● fix you   ● go to slēēp

4. what did the elephant do?

_____

    ● went to the shōw   ● went to slēēp

    ● went out   ● left

5. what did she see when she woke up?

_____

    ● one flȳ   ● many men

    ● lots of boys   ● many bugs

6. who took the elephant awāy? _____

    ● the flȳ   ● a girl   ● the bugs   ● a hound

7. they dropped her in the _____.

does he want these trēēs?

1. make a circle ō̄ver the word <u>he</u>.

2. make a box around the word <u>does</u>.

3. make <u>s</u> under the word <u>these</u>.

---

bill liked to jump. he would jump on the tāble. he would jump ō̄ver the ball.

one dāy he jumped on the dog. the dog barked at him so loud that bill ran and hid. so bill stopped jumping.

1. who liked to jump? _____

2. who barked at bill? _____

3. why did he stop jumping?

_____

- the dog barked at him.   ● the dog kissed him.
- the dog hid him.

---

1. make a <u>4</u> in the circle.

2. make a <u>3</u> next to the <u>4</u> .

3. make the word <u>in</u> under the <u>3</u> .

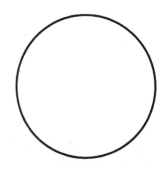

1. a girl had a pet _____.

       ● gōat   ● cōat   ● bōat   ● gate

2. the gōat ate cans, and he ate _____.

3. the gōat ate pans, and he ate _____.

4. the gōat ate capes, and he ate _____.

5. who saw the big red car nēar the house?

   the _____

       ● gōat   ● farmer   ● robber   ● robe

> if you shout, you must lēave.

1. make a <u>g</u> ōver the word <u>lēave</u>.

2. make a circle around the word <u>if</u>.

3. make a box under the word <u>shout</u>.

five elephants met on a rōad. one elephant said, "let's get rid of the bugs around here."

"yes," the other elephants said.

a bug said, "if you trȳ to get rid of us, we will send our best man after you. and our best man is a mouse."

the elephants ran so fast that they made a rōad ōver the hill.

1. how many elephants met on the rōad? _____

2. the elephants wanted to get rid of the _____.

3. who was the bug's best man? a _____

---

1. make the word <u>in</u> under the box.

2. make the word <u>ōver</u> in the box.

3. make the word <u>under</u> ōver the box.

1. whȳ was the girl's dad mad at the gōat?

the gōat _____.

    ● hit things   ● found things   ● ate things

2. what did the girl's dad have? a _____

    ● red gōat   ● red ēar   ● red car   ● white car

3. where were the girl and the gōat?

in the _____

4. whȳ did the car robber go flying?

the gōat _____.

    ● called   ● hit him   ● ate him   ● bit him

5. the girl's dad said, "that gōat

can _____ with us."

    ● fun   ● stāy   ● plāy   ● swāy

6. the robber said, "I am _____."

> when did you stop shouting?

1. make a box around the question mark.

2. cross out the word when.

3. make f under the word stop.

look at the picture on page 142 of your reader.

1. does the girl look happy or sad? _____

---

there was a flying goat. the goat kept flying into things. the goat said, "I can fly, but I can't see very well."

a mouse said, "I can't fly, but I can see. let me sit on your back and tell you where to go."

now the flying goat does not fly into things.

1. who said, "I can fly, but I cannot see"?

_____

2. who said, "I can't fly, but I can see"?

_____

3. why did the goat fly into things?

_____

4. does the goat fly into things now? _____

5. who tells the goat where to fly?

_____

1. a girl named Jane wanted to flȳ, _____, _____.

2. what did she want to make? a _____
    ● flȳ   ● kite   ● bird   ● trēē

3. they made the kite out of _____

_____.

    ● pāper and wool   ● pāper and birds
    ● pāper and striñg and wood

4. Jane was all set to go, _____, _____.

5. but her father said, "_____, _____, _____."

_____

┌──┐
│   │
│   does she have our cōats?   │
│   │
└──┘

1. make a circle around the question mark.

2. make a v under the word does.

3. cross out the word our.

look at the picture on page 144 of your rēader.

1. is Jane's kite big or small? _____

2. is her father standing or sitting? _____

---

      a lādy had a little car that would not go.
it would not go bēcause it was in the mud.
      an elephant came to the lādy and said, "if
you will give me some nuts, I will help get your
car out." so the lādy gave the elephant some nuts,
and the elephant got the car out of the mud.

1. who had a little car? _____
       ● an elephant   ● a lādy   ● a man

2. whȳ didn't the little car go?

_____

3. did the elephant help the lādy? _____

4. what did the lādy give the elephant? some _____

1. who wanted to flȳ? _____
        • jan   • her dad   • jane   • pane

2. where did jane go when she held on to the kite?

into the _____
        • skȳ   • water   • house   • barn

3. when she was ōver the town, she said, "I want

to go _____, _____, _____."

4. how far from town did the kite land? five

_____
        • dāys   • yēars   • miles   • fēēt

5. did jane ever trȳ flȳiñg again? _____

| do you want to go with us? |

1. cross out the word <u>do</u>.

2. make a box around the question mark.

3. make a box around the word <u>go</u>.

look at the picture on page 147 of your reader.

1. is jane holding a kite or a cloud?

_____

2. does she look happy or sad? _____

3. is she looking up or down? _____

_____

      a kite said, "I think I will fly up in the sky."
so the kite went up and up.

      five clouds said, "what are you doing up here,
kite? can't you see that we are having a meeting?"

      the kite said, "I can stay here if I want."

      the clouds said, "and we can make rain if
we want."

      so the clouds made so much rain that the kite
went back to the ground.

1. who said, "I think I will fly up in the sky"?

_____

2. who said, "what are you doing up here?"

_____

3. what did the clouds make to get rid of the kite?

_____

1. the little cloud lived in the _____.

  ● skȳ   ● park   ● barn   ● sēa

2. he lived with his _____.

  ● mother and brother   ● father and brother
  ● father and mother

3. who was the best rāin
   māker in the skȳ? the _____

  ● father cloud   ● mother cloud
  ● brother cloud   ● little cloud

4. whȳ did the little
   cloud fēēl sad? _____

  ● he couldn't slēēp   ● he couldn't māke rāin
  ● he couldn't swim

5. whȳ did the little cloud go far from his mother and

   father? _____

  ● he was sad.   ● his father made loud sounds.
  ● there was no rāin.   ● a wind bēgan to blōw.

---

we dōn't have a very big car.

1. cross out the word dōn't.

2. make a circle around the word car.

3. make a y ōver the word we.

look at the picture on page 150 of your reader.

1. what are the mother cloud and the father cloud making? _____

2. does the little cloud look happy or sad? _____

3. which cloud is darker, the little cloud or the father cloud? _____

---

a rock was in love with a tree. but the tree was tall and the rock was small. then one day, the wind began to blow very hard. the wind bent the tree down to the ground. when it came near the rock, the rock gave the tree a kiss.

1. who was in love with a tree? _____

2. what bent the tree down to the ground? _____

3. what did the rock give to the tree? _____

4. who was tall, the tree or the rock? _____

1. how many tēars came out when the little cloud trīed

    to crȳ? _____
    - lots   - none   - one   - some

2. the small dēēr and the mother dēēr werₑ _____.
    - trippₑd   - proud   - trappₑd   - runniñg

3. could his mom and dad hēar the little cloud? _____

4. when the cloud bēgan to shake,

    he became _____.
    - bigger and darker   - smaller and shŏrter
    - smaller and darker

5. what did the dēēr sāy? "_____."
    - stop that   - wē're wet   - go awāy   - thank you

6. the mother cloud was very _____.
    - loud   - proud   - pound   - little

    ┌─────────────────────────────┐
    │   │
    │   nell sat on a log.   │
    │   │
    └─────────────────────────────┘

1. make a box around the word <u>log</u>.

2. make a line under the word <u>on</u>.

3. circle the word that tells who sat on the log.

look at the picture on page 153 of your reader.

1. how many deer are in the picture? _____

2. do the clouds look happy or sad? _____

3. who is making rain? _____

---

tim wanted to go for a swim. but the sky was dark with clouds. tim was sad. an old man said, "don't feel sad about the clouds in the sky. they will bring rain." so tim ran in the rain and had a good time.

1. who wanted to go for a swim? _____

2. what was in the sky? _____

3. who was sad? _____

4. who said, "don't feel sad about the clouds"?

_____